Published by Flowerpublishing
©2018 Robert Bergeron

Painter Pierre Morin

Bookcover design

ISBN 978-1-927914-89-2

All rights reserved. No part of this book may be reproduced, stored in a retrieval system or transmitted in any form or by any means without the prior written permission of the publisher, except by a reviewer

who may quote brief passages in a review to be printed in a newspaper, magazine or journal

Flowerpublishing

www.flowerpublish.com

Montreal Canada

This book is dedicated to my two kids John and Sopheia

Where imagination should be encouraged and dreamed about

Rhymes is like life if it doesn't make sense it doesn't matter if it rhymes

Work hard, sing, be good to others and don't forget love is the most important word

Be smart, hear, listen, understand and then decide

Poetry, Poverty And Peace Rhymes

Battle Within 10

Pain 11

Think 12

Desire 13

Passion 14

Will 15

Decision 16

Lazy Mind 17

Action 18

Giving 19

Celebrity 20

Feelings 21

Believe 22

Needs 23

Terrible 24

Inexplicable 25

Tired 26

Share 27

Not a match 28

A Wish 29

Reaction 30

Pride 31

Faith 32

Dedication 33

Judgement 35

Path 37

In the wrong 38

Stretch 40

Hurt 41

Influence 42

Selfworth 43

Diamond 44

Lost 45

Regret 46

Push 47

A real Doctor 48

Shine 50

Explore 51

School 52

Meaning 54

Educated 55

Confidence 56

Grasp 57

Rush 58

Holding back 59

Ego 60

Class 61

Black and white 62

Control 63

Appreciated 64

Reason 65

Contentment 66

Abuse 67

Leader 68

Darkness 69

Fake 70

Sober 71

Sex 72

First 73

Speech 74

Balance 75

Move 76

Contradictory 77

Observation 78

Tongue 79

Black 80

Choice 81

Life 82

Unconditional 83

Strong 85

Confused 86

Consignment 87

Spiritual 89

Dizzy 90

Upset 91

Obnoxious 92

Procrastinating 93

Perfection 94

Battle Within

I'm fighting not to be a gangster
My heart's about to crack
The thin line about good and bad
I'm beyond feeling sad
I'm soon about to feel glad
I do not blame my dad
Everything I see makes me mad
She didn't use you because you're dumb
She used you because you couldn't hold together
A chain is only strong if it has no weak links
At the end it will sink
That's why you have to think
The smallest thing is as important
Cause if you feel small
You'll act shallow
You will not prosper you'll discourage
Don't be greedy no need to be needy
Did you get up to pee or party
I am no saint I'm stuck in paint
A perfect picture going nowhere

Pain

The clouds are not loud

The noise is in the crowd

Doesn't anybody bow

It's hard to be proud

They make me say ouch

I hardly say wow

I don't want to say ciao

Think

Conniving is a knife

Change can create hate

Interconnect the mind

There will always be crime

You should fight for peace

Not a piece of

What's not yours

But ours

Desire

I'm walking along the highway
Watching the cars pass me by
I start to wonder where they are going
They`re driving so fast
I hope there having a blast
It's the only way to last
Never ever forget about your past
Yesterday is what you learn tomorrow
All I need is for you to touch me
I don't like when you preach to me
I already had people teach me
Just want to say you pleased me
Every night I dream that you see me
Life's not always what it seems
The craziest feeling in the world is wanted
You'll end up being haunted
By The greatest fear
thinking you didn't get what you deserve
Became fat kept eating all of life's desserts
Full of unneeded things in your mind

Passion

We might not change

But the world will

If I could see the light

Would I be bright

Maybe possibly be right

Could my dreams be in my sight

Why does this life have to bite?

The only key is to fight

My only will is to write

Makes me fly high like a kite

It helps me enjoy the night

Will

I can be smart and not wise

It's up to me to rise

Lost it giving all that I had

and I'm still so glad

Sometimes acting bad

But ended up more sad

Cause I act like a wee little lad

Decision

I'm a poet and almost half of my life I did wrong

I'm thirty five I'm lost but about to be found

Cause I drowned in hate of this world

Full of blame but not my blame

But the shame that I was around

The sound that I heard

Was from a herd of lost souls

Without direction trying to get an erection

Whether it was sexual or not

But I fear not cause my intentions here so pure

Wanting to feel the blade

that came from the hand of god man or the devil

Lazy mind

Only death will tell the tale of history

Bullshit is in the ear of mankind

The mind cannot believe what it cannot see

That's why it's almost impossible to be free

If you had a choice money or friends

What would it be

It will come out of the rear

It's what you hold dear

Dining and winning

Action

You text

Touch less

Mind talking

Contact less

Tech specialist

Bored isolation

Creation some bad

Break up easy

Far many things to busy

Giving

I steal your beat to make harmony

I am a rapper I would love to tap her

Show no power get no respect

People wish I mind my business

Your strong you can do anything in this world

We all have the same weakness

I'm quiet and silent in my mind

I want to hear your voice I do have a choice

Celebrity

Tired of feeling wise alone

You don't share you don't care

Lend five dollars you just lost a friend

Get it I don't fucking pretend

Unfortunately, it's the new trend

People don't know how to blend

They're better off being greedy

Trust me they're very needy

They think they're very pretty

Forgot how to be cool

Instead they're just so cruel

They never heard the word divine

Just drink a lot of wine

What's important they will never find

It's a shame they're just so blind

Last thing on their mind is kind

Feelings

Until you become a master

You will be a bastard

I want to be famous

How could you blame us?

Don't want death

Just want faith

If you believe in yourself

I hate the word selfish

I will look down at you like a fish

I stopped appreciating a dish

I only think about what I wish

I think I'll end up rich

But I'm in a ditch

I will never forget

Life is a gift

Believe

Love is my only power

My only friend is earth

Death is my own expectation

Time is my only bore

Fear is my only weakness

Lust is my only dream

Giving is my own negativity

Crying is the only way

To make me feel like I am dying

Like reliving again

Needs

It's never too late to create

Never dwell on another's tale

I have a lot to tell

Look where I'm going

Cause I fell

Surrounded by hell

Terrible

Creation is dedication

There is no life without it

I will first fulfill your needs

But I'm next text

Don't fucking test

It's my turn now to feel your sex

Do your best I want to erect

Don't want to feel vexed

Her mouth makes me feel blessed

Tired of a test I am going to rest

I love her breast not depressed

I am a warrior not a worrier

Inexplicable

A shooting at a school is so cruel

Reminds us of a world so cold

Life is as evil as it is good

I guess that's the way it will always be

It's as bad as we let it be

It's only good with hard work

We work so hard for comfort

No more time for what is right

Until that time we care more for others

Things will never change

They'll always be so strange

Tired

Can you imagine how many have said it

And they truly don't get it

They can barely get laid

They think they'll join the raid

Not knowing they'll end up dead

Or crawling on their head

Do you truly know what's been said

Never ever forget that he has bleed

Leave me alone just go to bed

Understand what's been said

I do not think I'm better

I wrote it in this letter

All you have to do is climb the ladder

Share

Freedom isn't free

Its work at its hardest

We all need to see

What makes us bleed

The things we can be

You have to plant a seed

Try not to see greed

He holds all are deeds

I am free when I dream

I try not to sleep

Cause change seems to be steep

Only takes a great leap

To finally dream to be free

Life is a stream pretending to dream

Not a match

A hug is a touch

You make it or you break it

It's about what you seek

Don't be a freak

Have a drink

Even food can make you fat

Who has your back

Care only about your stack

Favors are the only savior

In this life or the next

Enjoy all the flavors

A wish

Two types of people
Passive or aggressive I'm both
passive listening to your bullshit
Aggressive when I can't take it no more
But I'm wrong should have left long ago
Living with you is like living in a storm
You hardly ever keep me warm
What's that poison in your heart
I tried to give you the world
All you did is make my feelings twirl
Would it be fun if you come
You're stuck and locked in a box
I tried so hard now I broke the crow bar
You wanting to be happy is so far
You'll find me at the bar

Reaction

What's your favorite dream
It's not always what it seems
I hope it's not about money
That would not be funny
My dream is to taste your honey
You gave back my confidence
You gave back my sweet emotions
For ever I would be blessed
Fed up with all the tests
Just want to rest in your arms
Like if there was no tomorrow
Don't forget life is borrowed
I will never dwell in sorrow
Your kiss is all I need
The only way to be free
Don't want to let you be
Just want you to see
I'm here for you forever

Pride

When all the war was finished

Rock and roll was torn threw blood and pain

Rock and roll are blood and pain

Power was given back to every soul

Freedom of speech is the greatest bitch

When people demand a change

I'm not wild I'm in style

Just been doing nothing for a long while

Just have to turn your dial

Faith

The world is a crazy place
Never let them slap you in your face
People use race thinking to find you a place
Too ignorant to know you're already at your place
Easy to believe in god too hard to do what's right
Everybody knows you'll fight
They are scared of your bite
Only death knows if you are bright
Cowards will never see the light

Dedication

Do it for the cries

Truthfully telling lies

The pain never dies

I dwell on thin air

I'm living on the line

I've never enjoyed my prime

I never took the time

But I shared a lot of rhymes

I understand all that crime

That's why you taste like lime

It's you hour to be sour

I wish I could be higher

I never wanted to hand out fliers

I just never finished school

I just wanted to be cool

And now I am paying the price

Once or twice I rolled the dice

All I was left with was some rice

Now I am on my knees screaming out to Christ

He says why cry your still alive

You have two feet to walk to the light

Two strong arms to hold me tight

I gave you mind to be bright

It's up to you to last the night

Ps I gave you two good eyes to see

What the hell is going on

Judgement

Adventure is like torture

I wanna fuck for kicks

I won't kill for tits

But I'll die for thrills

Pussy might give me chills

I don't care about big bill

That's why big bill likes to kill

Your mind gets me excited

Your thought make me die

That's why I will put you aside

And care more about power

Scream it out louder

Nothing else would make me prouder

I'll move threw you like water

Listening to you is like blowing up my bladder

Your will might be scattered

My heart will make sure you're shattered

I might die today but I am insured

My god ain't no bitch unlike you a snitch

A coward doesn't see it's at your reach

A loser thinks you need to be rich

That's why You end up in a ditch

That's why he created the leach

Path

I gotta take a stand

Cause I can't stand seeing you mad

Pretending you're alright

Pretending to be right

I am losing my sight for what is right

I can't remember a good night

The last time I had with you

Pain with you is being full of glue

Your attitude is really blue

Or maybe when you're just with me

Or that's the way you'll always be

The rate you're going you'll never be free

In the darkness out of the light

Hold on tight cause your falling fast

I keep on going with you now I can't last

You think because you have kids you can't have a blast

Trust me your wrong

I do my best but you think I`m like the rest

I do feel like a loser being with you

I guess I do drink a lot

I must be bored of you

You got to start being true

In the wrong

I love my kids

Pure true love I can't be a sinner

keep it simple   What am I doing

it is a delight try to keep it right

I can only offer you a hot meal

And to show you by example

Easy is the key read about everything

Studying is right way

As you read about the things that you read

Learn about the things that you need

One by one things become clearer

It is important to learn from your pears

Nothing more precious than working on your dreams

But unfortunately, you will have to earn it

Almost nothing comes to be free

Only then could you be able to see

Pride is all about not hiding

This world will take you for a ride

Fun is a must find something to believe in

Because there is no life without it

To be good is to live without many things

To be bad is to live with too many things

Balance is the all time goal for perfection and happiness

They say you'll get what you deserve

In this life or the next

Stretch

Money can only give you some satisfaction in life
Balance is key
I don't want to hear you plead
I don't want to see you bleed
It's too late to say please
Maybe you can change you lust of greed
You could do something great
But it's too hard to change your way
God gave you all these days
You had many chances to pray
He was listening to what you had to say
He does want you to be ok
You don't want your parents to teach you
But you blame god when things aren't easy
Life is always going to be greasy
A lot of people act sleazy Your story is very cheesy
When you didn't find contentment
You blew off many appointments
You didn't care about your statement
Life's a second compared to eternity

Hurt

There is no master don't be a bastard

We dream of heroes cause we got none

Forgot where you're from

Not pathetic I'm not dead yet

It always seems like we're almost there

Wear and tear do you really care

I don't think you dare

I know you won't share

Tried to buy many times

Trying to find what is mine

Influence

Evil does evil

The good should do well

They know what they want fear but no fear

Destiny for you not to far

You only have scars

Time for only a little prayer

Only if you dare

Not that many people care

Hardly nobody really shares

Most of the times things aren't fair

Always find time to play

Regardless of things they may say

Let it out let loose

Selfworth

I don't care about you

Just wanna take your soul

You will dwell in my shadow

I encourage you to be shallow

The more people I turn

The more I will win this battle

Hurry up and get on the saddle

I want to make you tremble

Only then you will do what I say

I`ll spoil you with temptation

Smother you with greed

Until you pay your deed

You will never be free

All make sure you don't see

Once you let me in

I will never let you be

I am the creator of hate and sinner

Diamond

My heart is like the nicest day
I would put myself in harm's way
I'm tired of doing nothing about it
I always wait until it's too late
Just want to find someone great
Always alone when it's time to eat
All I have is my two feet
Time to do something about it
Got to put your neighbours first
Just put away your hate
Time to do something great
Could be just talking to somebody
Or just giving some time

Lost

Why so sad

No need to be bad

I'll never understand

Life is like living on a beach

Everything is at your reach

Wish I didn't have to preach

Knowledge doesn't come free

We`re all dumb until we become one

To become one will only happen to some

It's not where you`re from it's what you become

We do drugs to become numb

We work too hard we forgot where were from

In reality we are just drones

Being chewed like a piece of gum

Regret

It's easy to blame the walk of fame

It's just a hall of shame for me

I saw them freezing

I saw them bleeding

And I didn't lead them

Until the light was in my sight

Telling me to do what's right

I'm ready to pay the price

To become one with Christ

He's not tough nor rough

But it's called sacrifice

To live without all the things we hold dear

Please don't lay out tears

Don't make the same mistake as are peers

I won't throw the first stone

I don't have it in my bones

I'm not the one sitting on the throne

I am just a simple man living without a plan

It's about time I take a stand

Got to protect all his land

Life is like living on the sand

Hoping to find our oasis

Push

Failure is wanting something too much

Why don't we know what happiness is

If the penalty is to high

Then everybody would lie

First take a second and sit on the grass

Before you become the biggest ass

You enjoy the shoe in your mouth

A real doctor

Without the man who cuts and stitches
The population today would be greatly smaller
Are parents would die a lot sooner
God bless the man who cuts and stiches
To really help is to truly be lonely
Because they know how it feels to save a life
To put ourselves first to the one who is dying
Is truly really impossible to the one that their heart is true
A real doctor knows practice makes perfection
Cause he knows not every life can be saved
At the end of their life they truly made a difference
Only if they understand what the title means
To be a real doctor he has to work real hard
In life he has to deal with all the cries
They did their best to the one who dies
Now god says it was their time to say goodbye
You did your best now I will heal all of their cries
Who cares about all the scares
they belong with the stars
They dedicated their lives to save lives
Truly bless the one who cuts and stitches
God gave me back my feet threw you

To give up is to throw in the towel to the devil

God need not make miracles

when we have people like you

God bless the one who cuts and stiches

If we don't believe why should he

If he don't believe why should we

Unfortunately, you have to get a grip on faith

God bless the ones who cuts and stitches

Shine

I've seen you

You can talk the talk

But can you walk the walk

Can you dance to this song

Can you sing to this song

Don't think you can play along

Can you remain strong

My actions scream louder than words

I am talking to all of you turds

Who cares about the truth when you're not truthful

Life can be fruitful

Been very soulless been very careless

Could have done anything I love to do

Explore

Life is about

My side your side and the beautiful truth

I wanna be a knight

Sex is a nice night

The world belongs to you it does belong to me

What are you going to do

Explore the world

Leave your print

Think about what you didn't

I insist to be free into the wild there I will be

Aren't I supposed to be here out of love and passion

And not for the lust of greed

That's why we do the deed

Don't matter why we`re here

Just want to have to be

School

Listen to the rules

Learn to be cool

Go to school

That's how you earn your tools

Well schools not for fools

When you know How to use it

Life is like rolling the dice

If you want to be paid the high price

If not come out with an ideal

Try to feel what he gave you

Don't drive by it try it

Don't cry just enjoy it

You do have a lot to prove

There is a lot to do

If you want to be true

There is no life without it

There is no way you can buy it

All you have to do is try it

Not everybody's bright

But we all have are rights

To live a life of might

Cowards never try it

They always try to buy it

It's easy to feel dirty

Life is wild

There is no time to wait for a while

Meaning

I wish it was what it seems

But it's only in my dreams

If you were mine you would find peace of mind

A life without crime

The only crime is the way that I feel

Learn what he gave you it will save you

I know you think it's true

I just wanna get through to you

I'm tired of feeling so blue

What is done today

Could be undone tomorrow

But it could be too late

It will be your fate

She might not be waiting at the gate

A crime is like a rhyme

If it's good enough you can make it

Educated

Holding power too long

That's when you become to sour

You've reached your hour

Greed is being too rich

That's when you became a bitch

Left me in a ditch

That's when I took a grip

Put my talent in a dip

Starting grabbing my dick

Words are life

That's when we earn our price

Confidence

My dick

Ashes to ashes dust to dust

If I don't use it it's going to rust

I don't want to see crust

I like feeling the rush

I do drugs to become numb

Cause I don't cum enough

My rhymes are clear that's what I hold dear

I am wild when I ride

Cause I know death can be tomorrow

Grasp

I write because I'm bright

It's the only thing in my sight

I wish I would bite

You do give me a fright

Always high like a kite

Do it before the end of the night

Rush

You're just a pain

Like a stain on my ass

You're worthless like brass

I'm worth gold cause I'm bold

You sold your mother long ago

Never did what you're told

Even you own girl says your cold

You truly lost your soul

Can't even please the ladies

Time you smoke a pound of grass

So you can feel something

Not just deal something

Holding back

You got to take it easy

Just don't make it to sleazy

You want me to die or rhyme

It's my time to live my prime

I don't believe in crime

Power is only for an hour

Tomorrow you could be living on the streets

Pretending you have a lot of beats

Big house nice cars

You'll end up with more scars then I will ever have

I listen to these songs

I don't know what they're saying

Seems like there blaming

Don't just try it defy it

Ego

Life is like a balance

You fill up one side

Faithfully he will fill up the other side

Not one soul greater than the other

He says it's time to change

Be loud be proud

Where's the love man

Joy is created by you

Not stuck in a tube

Class

Religion is good

When you show others how good it is

It's good when you do what you're told

It works when you don't sell your soul

Death is a friend to the warriors

A coward's worst enemy is death

Black and White

The month of thanksgiving

Is being driven

In back of the wheel

Depends on who is driving

Equal hearts there is none

Given needs no thanks

I hope my lords not a prank

Or else it's going to be sunk

We do all live in a tank

The most powerful word is thanks

Appreciate what has been given

It's what a good man needs to be driven

Strive and take no bribes

Money has no place in death

Without bold love

There is no month of thanks given

Control

My dearest mother

Not everybody can be bothered

To take care of my father

There is no other

Love from a brother

Just want to be heard

I am glad I was smothered

Thanks for the extra covers

Ready to be discovered time to hit the buzzer

Mother taught me not to slither

It's all about how you glitter

Never become bitter

Or else you'll end up in the gutter

Appreciated

Poetry about war

War makes me snore

It's getting old man

War can be bought at a store

War can be brought to a store

To them it's just a score

Rack em and stack them

I wish I can smack them

Are they doing crack man

They're about to be sacked

I doubt they'll remain in tacked

They get cracked like a tic tac

War can be an oar

A simple tool to cross a river

Most times there are warnings

Big waves along the way

Some will be torn

Some will be mourned

And some will be reborn

Is war here forever

Reason

Music is my melody

The hell you cannot see

Glory's not given to you

Earned in many ways

We had many days to foresee what I have seen

This isn't just another dream

To become what I have been

Working on my esteem

Boiling a lot of steam

How many smiles today

I am here no need to pray

Hopefully today is the day

What else can I say

You cut the best you'll be the rest

I bleed when drinking rum

Hoping not to become too dumb

Contentment

Embrace what we have

it isn't all that bad

No need to be sad

when you are that brave

When you're able to say that you gave

Feels good when you bathe

I got it all being cool hoping not to become a fool

Abuse

Watch out for all that toking

You'll end up broken

Covered in blood all soaking

Living a life choking

Your body will start aching

It will be too late to start asking

Next step will be going to jail

Living in a cell full of hell

You won't be able to bail

Sometimes it might feel impossible

Changing is like winning the lottery

I might be lazy I might be sleazy

Work hard on your farm

Nothing will do you harm

Except for the greedy man

All you have to do is ask for a hand

And they'll get lost in the sand

Leader

Jesus had to bleed to lead us

Teach us how to be free

To live a life without greed

I guess he paid his deeds

At the end he didn't want to leave us

All he wanted to do is free us

Try to be more humble

Try not to stumble

He just wanted to save us

The world can be cruel

But I've seen some sights

That can lift your soul so high

But you got to work so hard

If it wasn't for that smile

I would have lost my mind years ago

Darkness

Tears come from fear

Sadness compressed

Pain is a strain

Blame has its part

Life is art

Tears I could do with out

Does nothing to shout

I tried to win the bought

I know how to cry

Almost made me die

Tired of them prying

I wanna stop crying

Everything ends up dying

Fake

True happiness is a lie

When you're a true liar

Truly happy truly blessed

This life is a test

Seems most are pests

To busy to be the best

We become like the rest

Chipped or perfect

Sober

Beer I hold dear

I love to cheer

I haven't found my career

Trying to find harmony

A drunk without a slam dunk

It's like feeling like a Twinkie

Life is a vibe live with pride

I'd rather die than to be shy

Opportunity I have none

I'd rather enjoy the beer

It's what I hold deer

Sex

I look in your eyes

I see burning roses

I am thinking of so many poses

My skin starts to sweat an itch I need to scratch

As my words find a way through your heart

Are senses start to feel uncontrollable emotions

As are touches seem to want to come closer

As are lips seem to come in close

That first kiss makes me feel bliss

As our lips wet all around are necks

My hand comes closer to your lower lips

Raising up your skirt giving rest to your lips

I use my face to caress your breast

I pray this isn't another test

I use my hands to rub your chest

I was going to kiss your lower lips

But instead you grabbed my seed maker

Pointing it closer to your life maker

That first penetration made me see that bliss again

I lean over you for that great kiss

As your hand touches me in the right place

My dream came true using your face

Feel not out of place neither any disgrace

First

Speak your mind now or forever hold your peace

Till death does us a part

Power means success

But not the power you suspect

Far beyond your mind can imagine

The eternity of travel time and space

What only the eyes can see

So far away to the goal

Perfection is unachievable

But desire is unstoppable

Passion and all its glory

It's too late to say you're sorry

Act today fear not your fears

Brother it doesn't end here

Now lift your glass and cheer

God knows I love my beer

I work today now I have to play

Speech

Words are not just words

Its are essentials nothing less

A touch is a must

A kiss is bliss

Being happy is the only quest

Fear is the only weakness

Dreams are for us to rest

Give it all your best

Balance

You're eatable and incredible

Chewable and gullible

Not brought up with true manners

You're lost in all the banners

Never too late to change

Never ever live in blame

Or else it will be a shame

Nothing should ever be the same

I don't want to rule

Just want to be cool

I'm not going to drown in a pool

If you lose your heart

Animal without class

Just a guy living a lie

Bothered to be discovered

Where there is love there is power

When alone there is desire

Time to change when things are strange

Everybody gets a second chance

I'm a predator not an editor

Move

Every breath is a test

Every touch is lust

Working is a must

Don't sit on your butt

Listen to your gut

Or else you'll get cut

Fun is a must

Just don't get bust

If you don't move you'll rust

Getting out there is a rush

Be aware of who to trust

Contradictory

I have a heart but it's cut

I have soul but it's injured

I have will but no desires

I have power but no strength

I love but live in hate

I'm weak but very powerful

I care but can't be bothered

Not afraid to die but scared to live

Full of action but no plan

I have life but I'm not living

I live without fear but I'm scared

I love but can't let go

My mind is busy but I'm lonely

The world brings me joy but I'm in pain

What have you done today

Observation

Rain drops dripping on flower petals

Wind breathing on my skin on a hot day

A nice bath after a nice days work

A kiss from the one who we love

The bees working hard to provide us honey

The sun drying me up after a nice swim

Good words come after nice actions

To climb that mountain to become one with the sight

To teach my kids what my elders could not

To teach myself what my father could not

While I lie on the grass a butterfly lands on my nose

While I sleep my dreams come true

Who says this isn't a beautiful world

Tongue

The power of are great sensations

As I hold you firmly

As my tongue reaches over that lumpy surface

That wet feeling on my lips

Sometimes dripping down my chin

As my tongue twirls around

Stroking up and down

Bold enough to stick my tongue in to it

I can't believe one lick can do so much

My body feels a feeling of joy

All that excitement and energy that one lick can give

They don't all have the same taste

But none the less satisfying

Refreshing all the way to the mind

Oh lord I ask for just one thing

God when I die

Make sure there is plenty of ice cream for me

Black

As I seal the deal that dwells in darkness

Hides behind the light

The most forgotten place in space

Far behind any disgrace

Caring only about their own race

Obviously way out of place

Just staring at his face

I don't just rhyme

I rape the lies hiding behind the truth

Latching on to others fears

Using self pity to gain control of the city

Fuck it I won't have any pity

For you or your unrealities

You're a test hell no you're a pest

I will send you back to the west

You are just like the rest

Choice

I never want to be cold again

I never want to be alone anymore

I finally fixed my sword today

And I'm not going to pray

Because today is are destiny

With the power in are hands

I have to stop being pulled down

I never want to be frowned upon

I'm not going to drown in a pound

I have felt the meaning of life

Half the time it makes me cry

At a point I just wanna die

Obviously I start crying

Life is made of worthy hearts

Many have died for are future today

Doesn't matter how much you pray Tell god I say hey

We need this hell for heaven to become reality

Practically living a good life

Uncertain the goals of are life

Read his book and study hard

For there the answer lies

Got to make good with him before you die

Now it's time for me to say good bye

Life

Your mother left you to the wolves

Now you're truly all alone

Cold world what have you learned

Passion always has its turn

Chooses the ones that are most worthy

Trust that bond you can't brake

Proud of who you are

Hell knocking on my door

Even if I say don't what's the point

Feeling like I do

Wish we could see wish we could heal

What is are deal

Will we see this thing of life

Or will it not come to us I do not know

Tearing us apart peace by peace

Still don't know why that is why I cry

Too early to say good bye

What is reason I was accused of treason

Passion give me a couple of lashes

Unconditional

I could give the world to somebody and still end up alone

My destiny the crappiest

but sometimes the most rewarding

The stuff we know and do

When I get fed up I will kill

But I didn't say what

Kill is a word just like any other

Could be your feelings deal with it mother fucker

I wish I could be a trucker

Visit the world so many things to see

when you're not drowning

Frowning is bullshit learn your fucking language

be proud

Evil or not I will succeed I did plant my fucking seed

I really do like to breed

Feels good truth or dare

Look in the mirror killing is not for sure but it is there

There won't be any time for one last prayer

And they say it's not good to swear

Depends when you are saying it

Anger you won't catch me in jail

I will bail before the possibility

Doesn't mean I'm not there

Struggling with what deal or no deal

All you know is to steal

So far away from enlightenment might as well stone you

Because everybody knows you froze

hope you're not to stoned

Sooner or later you will be just bones

Cold as the universe

Intrust in me and all will be forgiven

Won't deprive you with nothing

But you do have to come with something

It's called mother fucking talent

Fear or no fear it is a delight it is really bright

If you don't doze off in twilight

Never lose your sight

you have to become one with might

Before the end of the night

Strong

I'd rather be flying on a boat
Then floating in my mind
I wanna drive a five point o
Not get arrested by five o
I'd rather get fucked by pussy
Then getting fucked by a bitch
Living a life riding
Not a life fucking dying
Tired of fucking hiding
I'm not going to start crying
I don't care if she calls me a prick
I'm going to start using my dick
Three fucking layers thick
I will try not to think
Or nail myself to the wall
You will never see me crawl
Only on the way to her pussy
Or squeezing my penis in
You'll never find my next of kin
Or catch me doing a fucking sin
Aiguiser come un crayon de mine

Confused

The only rights we have

I'm not free to look   I might get slapped

I have the right to think   but the again

If I think too much   I'll end up in prison

I'm free to talk   I might get shocked

I'm free to walk   I might get shot

I guess all I really got   is my cock

When I think about it   not got a lot

Or a really good plot

I'm stuck with all the sluts

At the end I might get dropped

That's why my mind gets popped

Navy seals that's the real deal

Pussy is the greatest thrill

Riding gives me chills

You don't need the pills

I will take your mind and put it on the grill

Only James bond could bail

Consignment

My mind is living in a cell
I ended up in jail
Surrounded by hell
Never been drunk and sober
My dreams got clobbered
Living with all the robber's
Don't look in my eyes
I will turn you up and down
Around and on the ground
You'll never be found
Some will say you drowned
I don't care if you're brown
Just want to earn my crown
Better not make a sound
The dirt will be calling your name
Crying to find someone to blame
Everybody knows your lame
Changing to all these wings
I'm moving like the wind
Drugs I hope they bring
Hope my mind loses track of time

So, I can just a few good rhymes

A snitch is harder to find

When moving to all these cells

Spiritual

What makes your religion better

Why isn't love enough

We should be fighting to get together

not pretending are way is better

If we truly believed in equality

the walls would have been torned down

The pen is not mightier than the sword

The truth is

Billions of religious people in the world

And still peoples shit stinks

Find me a word better then love

Plato said the secret to happiness is

To focus all your energy not on fighting the old

But on building the new

Dizzy

Love is like a ship

Could be a very rocky trip

Not all have the greatest pick

Wanting a good relationship

Sometimes you need to be whipped

Putting your heart in a dip

A candy that you lick

Two ways to use your lips

It's like being drunk and tipsy

To make it work be witty

True love is very pretty

If you don't share it will be shitty

If it ends it is a pity

When you're lost go to the city

You know it's real when you feel giddy

God bless the one called Aphrodite

Upset

You think you're blessed covered in sex
Selling your body letting evil win the bet
A dream is caused by what's been seen
Stop fighting against what you should be
Letting go will set you free
Life is like becoming a tree
Flowers become honey made by bees
Air being created by the leaves
Evil is like a dog with fleas
The world will die if we flee
A fish venturing in the great sea
A shark who tried to eat me
Humble yourself and take a nee what
Before you get cut up like meat
Become a soul with an amazing beat
Never ever accept defeat

Obnoxious

Man tries to control the world

Thinking he's a great lord

With too much money he became bored

Living only for what's in his hoard

When he dies he will mourn

The only gift we have was to be born

Greed hurts like a thorn

Now you've been warned

More Important to keep your neighbor warm

To master life is to find your perfect form

Many times, you made a terrible storm

Someone someday will rip off your horns

Time to think about being reborn

Procrastinating

Loves not an option
When the world is dying
Can't you see them crying
Super powers I wish I had
No more chances I'm getting mad
Too much waiting I'm getting fat
No one has my back
Brilliance is what you lack
You're sitting on a stack of bills
Feeding yourself with all those pills
You should just stop and chill
Ego is something you should let go
Need to start working on your soul
Eventually your spirit will glow
Stop thinking you need it more

Perfection

Love is the clay that holds us together
Everybody thinks their way is better
Thousands of years later
We are still like the weather
History has been handed down from the letter
Lust isn't always something you can trust
I have thought about it and it's up to us
Most souls can't handle the rush
Working hard to be happy is a plus
Needy people created a path for aching
The ones who feel in fear are the first ones to sing
We honor the ones we love with a ring
Devils jobs destroying good human beings
A struggle tortures differently every soul
A coward always wishes to live until he's old
Brought up thinking he should not be bold
Imagine a life where no man's heart is cold
Destiny seeking a path that can't be undone
Don't dwell on stories where you are from
You'll be destroyed when you think you've won
Not knowing it's all about what you have become

www.ingramcontent.com/pod-product-compliance
Lightning Source LLC
Chambersburg PA
CBHW032006220426
43664CB00005B/163